Lett

MW01099109

-ea, -en, -et

SCHOOL PUBLISHERS

Photos:
p. 2, bed © Harcourt Index; p. 3, ten © Superstock; p. 7, net © Veer; p. 4, © Shutterstock; p. 5, © Shutterstock; p. 6, © Harcourt Telescope; p. 8, © Superstock.

Printed in China

ISBN 10: 0-15-358379-7
ISBN 13: 978-0-15-358379-7

Ordering Options
ISBN 10: 0-15-358355-X (Grade K Below-Level Collection)
ISBN 13: 978-0-15-358355-1 (Grade K Below-Level Collection)
ISBN 10: 0-15-360632-0 (package of 5)
ISBN 13: 978-0-15-360632-8 (package of 5)

4 5 6 7 8 9 10 0940 15 14 13 12 11 10 09

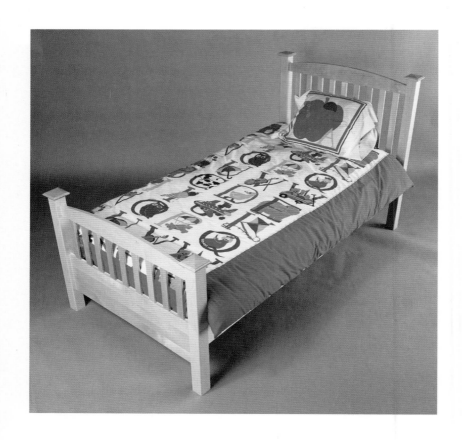

bed

ten

hen

red

pen

net

men